Praise for *The Pha*

"When you're finished with *The Pharmacist's Mate*, you experience something, and it's more than mere shifts of time. It's got spine and an itchy curiosity."
—*Austin American Statesman*

"In clean simple prose that is as powerful as it is spare, *The Pharmacist's Mate* weaves together life and loss, the story of a wanted pregnancy, and a mourned father. It's impossible not to surrender to Amy Fusselman's lovely haunting voice and strange meditations."
—Amanda Davis

"In this memorable, beautifully structured book, she gives us more than ironic asides or a catalog of her pop-culture interests (although she supplies those, too); she makes the world strange again, a place where dying and making life are equally mysterious and miraculous activities."
—*Time Out New York*

"Amy Fusselman's book will inspire those who want to be parents but still want to be cool. *The Pharmacist's Mate* is the book equivalent of independent garage rock—and that's a compliment."
—Neal Pollack, author of *The Neal Pollack Anthology of American Literature*

PENGUIN BOOKS

THE PHARMACIST'S MATE

Amy Fusselman's writing has appeared in
McSweeney's, *ARTNews*, and *Jane*. She lives in
New York City with her husband and son.

THE PHARMACIST'S MATE

by

AMY FUSSELMAN

———

PENGUIN BOOKS

PENGUIN BOOKS

Published by the Penguin Group
Penguin Putnam Inc., 375 Hudson Street,
New York, New York 10014, U.S.A.
Penguin Books Ltd, 80 Strand, London WC2R 0RL, England
Penguin Books Australia Ltd, 250 Camberwell Road,
Camberwell, Victoria 3124, Australia
Penguin Books Canada Ltd, 10 Alcorn Avenue,
Toronto, Ontario, Canada M4V 3B2
Penguin Books India (P) Ltd, 11 Community Centre,
Panchsheel Park, New Delhi – 110 017, India
Penguin Books (N.Z.) Ltd, Cnr Rosedale and Airborne Roads,
Albany, Auckland, New Zealand
Penguin Books (South Africa) (Pty) Ltd, 24 Sturdee Avenue,
Rosebank, Johannesburg 2196, South Africa

Penguin Books Ltd, Registered Offices:
Harmondsworth, Middlesex, England

First published in the United States of America by McSweeney's Books 2001
This edition with a new afterword published in Penguin Books 2002

1 3 5 7 9 10 8 6 4 2

Illustration on page 1 by Marcel Dzama

LIBRARY OF CONGRESS CATALOGING IN PUBLICATION DATA
Fusselman, Amy.
The pharmacist's mate / by Amy Fusselman.
p. cm.
ISBN 0 14 20.0235 6 (pbk.)
I. Title.
PS3606.U86 P48 2002
813'.6—dc21   2002072832

Printed in the United States of America

RKF

THE PHARMACIST'S MATE

1.

Don't have sex on a boat unless you want to get pregnant. That's what my friend Mendi's sailor ex-boyfriend used to tell her.

I want to get pregnant. Or maybe more accurately, I don't want to die without having had children.

I was a child once, with a dad. My dad is dead now. He died two weeks ago. I have never had anyone so close to me die. I am trying to pay attention to what it feels like.

I know it's early, but I keep thinking he's still here. Well, not here, I know he's not here, but on his way here. On his way back here from somewhere. Coming here.

Of course, I don't think it's my old dad in his old body coming here. It's my old dad, in a new form.

Thinking your dad might be coming in a new form is not so bad. It's like you're always excited, and getting ready, and listening for the door.

2.

The big problem I have had in trying to get pregnant is that I don't ovulate. Thus, I don't get my period. I mean, I can go six months.

I don't know why this is. And after a million tests at the gyno, they don't seem to know why either. Everything looks OK.

My theory is that I am stopping myself from having my period. I am doing this with my brain. I don't know how I am doing it, but I am doing it. And I am doing it because as much as I want to get pregnant, I am also very afraid.

3.

Before my dad was a dad, he was a guy on a boat in a war. This was World War II.

My dad had been studying pre-med at Virginia Military Institute. He had enlisted in the Army in 1944, but after a few months they discharged him because, my dad told me, "They didn't know what they were doing with medical students." So my dad went back to school for a while, until my grandfather called him up from Ohio and said people at home were starting to talk, and they were saying my dad was studying pre-med just to get out of serving. My dad told me that's when he said the hell with it, and signed up for the Merchant Marine. This was in the fall of 1945. He was twenty-one.

My dad was the Purser-Pharmacist's Mate on the Liberty Ship *George E. Pickett*. He kept a log from his first eight months at sea. He wrote a lot about his work.

Sample:

> Chief Steward came to me today with a possible case of gonorrhea. I'm going to wait until tomorrow to see how things turn out. Had him quit handling the food, at least.

It's funny to read things like that, because my dad never became a doctor. After the war, he went back to school and got his MBA.

4.

Sometimes I think this problem with children is something that runs in my family. My brother, who lives in Houston and is ten years older than me, had a problem with children fifteen years ago. He was in Ohio visiting my parents (I was away at school), when all of a sudden the phone rang. It was his live-in girlfriend, telling him she had just had two babies, a boy and a girl. Twins.

My parents didn't even know she was pregnant. My brother flew back to Houston. The next thing my parents heard, they had given the infants up for adoption.

The whole thing was so shrouded in weirdness and secrecy that several years after it happened I called my brother just to make sure that it was true. Because all I knew was what I had heard from my parents.

And my brother had said yes, it was true. He sounded pained. My brother and I are not very close. I didn't ask him more than that.

Another thing: my brother has a job selling high-tech sonar equipment to clients like the Navy, equipment they use to do things like search for John F. Kennedy Jr.'s plane.

And another: I have always wondered if someday these kids might show up on our doorstep.

5.

I am trying to get pregnant with Frank. Frank is my husband. He is 6'4". My dad was 5'7". Frank and my dad got along. Even though Frank's full name is Frank, my dad always gave his name two extra syllables, and said it sing-song, "Frank-a-lin."

Frank and my dad were both born and raised in Youngstown, Ohio. When they got together they liked to talk about the town landmarks, Market Street and Mill Creek Park, places I didn't know because I grew up around Cleveland.

And it never came up in conversation, but long ago, even before I was born, my dad had made arrangements to be buried in the cemetery at the end of Frank's street: Forest Lawn.

6.

I want to talk to my dad, but my dad is dead now. I know we can't have a regular conversation so I am trying to stay open to alternatives. I am trying to figure out other ways we can communicate.

Right after my dad's funeral, I came back to New York for a week of visits to the high-end fertility doctor. I had just started with the high-end fertility doctor, after nine months of getting nowhere with the low-end one.

I needed a week of visits to have my follicles monitored. I had just taken five days' worth of clomiphene citrate, a drug that tricks your pituitary gland into producing extra FSH (follicle stimulating hormone) and LH (luteinizing hormone), two natural gonadotropins that encourage follicle growth.

A follicle-monitoring appointment at the high-end fertility doctor involves the following: getting there between seven and nine a.m.; putting your name on a list; waiting until the nurse calls your name; going and getting your blood taken; returning to the waiting room with your arm bent around a cotton ball; waiting for the nurse to call your name again; and when she does, going to the examination room to lie on the table with your pants off so one of the ever-changing array of attractive, resident physicians can stick the ultrasound probe in your vagina to measure how big the follicle is. You need a follicle to get to eighteen millimeters before they will give you the shot of hCG (human chorionic gonadotropin) to make the follicle burst and release the egg.

After four mornings of this, a resident told me that one follicle, on my left side, had hit eighteen. So they gave me the shot, and then the next day, I was inseminated.

And I was sure when it was over that I was pregnant, because unlike all the other times I had taken clompihene citrate, and been shot with hCG, and been inseminated, this time I was doing it with my dad being dead. And I was sure my dad would be trying to help me out.

But the morning I was supposed to take my pregnancy test, I got my period.

7.

1/31/46: Eight days have now been spent in port at Pier 15 Hoboken, NJ. Ship still remains unassigned and unloaded. Vessel is of the Liberty type and called the *George E. Pickett*. It is manned and operated by the Waterman SS Co AT 0625. On 1/26 an adjoining vessel struck us and wrecked the No. 4 lifeboat davit. Hell of a racket. The crew is not a bad lot, but always clamoring for advances on their wages. The "Old Man," A.C. Klop, a Hollander by birth, is as tight with money as they come. There are many bets being made among the crew as to our port of destination, but it still remains a secret.

The ship is undergoing repair now, which it badly needs. Has been dry-docked, scraped and painted. All guns and mountings have been removed.

The previous voyage was to Yokohama, Japan, and lasted seven months. Some of the original crew remained for this voyage, but very few.

I am determined to learn to navigate, and study a little geography. Knowledge of both these subjects very poor.

8.

Before my dad died I saw the world as a place. By place I mean space. Fixed. Space did not move, but people moved in space. People and space could touch each other, but not very deeply.

After he died, I saw that people and space are permeable to each other in a way that people and people are not. I saw that space is like water. People can go inside it.

9.

My dad loved guns, loved them. My mom told me that when she and my dad were dating, he drove with a Luger lying in the space between their seats. Part of me chalks this up to the fact that my dad went to military school, then war. Part of me thinks he was living in a different time. Part of me isn't sure.

My father was in the hospital for six weeks before he died. When it became clear that his condition was really serious, my brother came home. One of the first things my brother did was roam around the house, searching for the guns. My mother had never wanted anything to do with them, and didn't even know where they all were stored.

My brother found three automatics, a revolver, and two rifles. He couldn't find the old Luger, though he said he knew my dad still had it.

He unloaded the guns. Then he laid them all out in a long row, on my dad's dresser:

> one stainless steel Walther PPK .380 caliber
>   automatic
> one stainless steel Seacamp .32 caliber automatic
> one blued steel Colt .380 caliber automatic
> one titanium Smith & Wesson .22 caliber revolver
>   with laser target
> one Armalite .22 caliber survival rifle
> one .30 caliber M-1 carbine

When I saw all the guns like that, rounded up from their hiding places and disassembled, the semi-automatics and rifles separated from their clips, the revolver emptied of its bullets, that's when I started to know that my dad wasn't going to live much longer.

10.

2/16/46: Well, I'm as salty a sailor as they come now. We have had the worst possible weather these last three days. It can't get any worse. As far as seasickness, I guess I'm immune to it. My stomach felt a little squeamish the first two days but it is all over now. I can eat just as regularly as on land. It is good to feel the roll of the ship under your feet, and these Liberties roll more than any cargo ship afloat, since they are almost flat on the bottom. We were having a 36° roll last night.

Had a fellow receive two nail punctures in his foot in the steering engine room. Couldn't do much about it. Opened it up and put sulfathiazole creme in it, and gave him a tetanus shot. I couldn't remember whether to give it subcutaneous or intravenous. Gave it sub-q and hoped for the best. At least I got it in. Looked it up in *Christopher's Minor Surgery* later and found out I gave it right. It's just an accident that I happened to have the antitoxin with me. I was so darn busy in port that I was going to let it go and take a chance by not having it. I just happened to be down near the WSA warehouse so I took the time to pick it up. It's a good thing.

11.

What is it about my dad being dead that I can't say it enough? That I feel like My Dad Is Dead would be a good name for my son?

That I can picture myself saying, "I can't talk right now, I have to pick My Dad Is Dead up from hockey?"

Singing, "Happy birthday to you, happy birthday to you, happy birthday dear My Dad Is Dead"?

I look My Dad Is Dead up on Yahoo! and discover that there is a band with that name. And they're from Ohio, like my dad, like me. And I can listen to their song right now, a noisy, static-y MP3 called "Don't Look Now."

12.

My dad is invisible. Everything invisible is interesting to me now. Like when I sit in the apartment we just moved into, and play guitar. When I sit here and am aware, as I play and sing, that the music is invisible. And I imagine what I would look like to a deaf person. That I would look like someone opening and closing her mouth and sliding one hand along some wood and using the other to touch some strings. And how that doesn't look like much. Just someone sitting, making little movements. Little patterns with the mouth, open close, open close, little patterns with the hand, up and down, up and down. And how the only way a deaf person would know what I was doing is because the movements are creating vibrations. And how even though the vibrations are invisible, I can feel them in the air. I can feel them, they are there, they are as there as I am.

I have always thought that seeing a band play in a bar is more interesting theater than most plays in theaters. The guitarist standing there, wiggling the fingers, and making the giant vibrations, is about hundred times more poetic and mysterious than someone in a costume saying words they memorized, words that are supposed to be About Something.

But I say that and then I also have to admit that when I am at home playing guitar and singing, I am playing and singing a song I wrote when I was in college, in a band that played in bars. And the song is called "I Love My Mom," and we played it loud and fast:

> *I love my mom*
> *I love my mom*
> *She's no sex bomb*
> *But she's my mom*
> *She sends me food*

When I am gone
She's old, she's cool my mom rules

I love my dad
I love my dad
I am so glad
That he's my dad
He sends me money
Even though I'm bad
He's old, he's cool, my dad rules

And on one level the song was supposed to be funny, because even though it had sweet lyrics, we played it like a rant. But on another level it wasn't funny at all, because at the time I wrote it I was mad as hell at my mom and dad, and the song was like an imitation of how I was loving them then, through clenched teeth.

And now, when I sing the song, I remember specifically how I held my dad's hand and sang it to him in the hospital, two days before he died.

13.

2/18/46: Our destination was changed by radio today. We are going to Saint Lazaire in France to unload and possibly pick up French war brides. The crew nearly went crazy when they heard there might be women on board. Little do they realize that it will become a pain in the neck. Won't be able to cuss, and will probably have to come to the table dressed up. I took an awful kidding at the table today, because they said I would have to act as "midwife" in case any of the passengers were pregnant.

14.

Yesterday morning I went back to the fertility doctor for follicle monitoring. I have taken my five days' worth of clomiphene again. This is the fifth time I have taken it. I did it three times with the low-end fertility doctor, and now I've done it twice with the high-end one.

You aren't supposed to take clomiphene too many times, because it's terrible for you. So this, the fifth time, is the last time I can take it. After this, I go on to the next, more aggressive treatment: shots.

I am scared of shots. So I was hoping, when I went in yesterday, that the ultrasound would find many large follicles. But there were only two of them, and they were small. One was ten millimeters, and one was twelve.

15.

Air is very interesting now. I can spend a long time sitting in my apartment, looking at the air.

Yesterday I was at the gym, on the elliptical trainer. I was thinking about my uterus. My uterus which, I have read, is almost infinitely expandable. And I was picturing my uterus, with its lining of blood, empty except for once-a-month when the microscopic egg bobs around in it like a single life preserver in the ocean.

And then I was picturing the dots and dashes of sperm, like the sudden eruption of a ship's SOS.

And I was thinking how strange it is that these tiny circles and lines Ping-Ponging around my uterus are powerful enough to burst into a life.

And as I was thinking this it was like a door opened, and I looked up and thought, my dad is here. And I looked up at the air in front of my elliptical trainer, the air that did not look like anything unusual, that just looked like regular air hanging out between people and things, and I said, hi dad, without using my voice, and I smiled.

And then I was excited and felt like I had to say a lot of things at once, like I love you and I miss you and I am writing about you, can you help me with it? And as I said that I was smiling, because I knew my dad would be sort of rolling his eyes and smiling at that, like he's dead, and I'm asking him to help me with my homework.

And after a while I felt like my dad was gone and I didn't talk to him anymore, just kept moving my legs in the up-hill egg shape, like I already had been doing the whole time.

16.

When my dad first went into the hospital, we didn't think he was going to die. He just had a bad cold, which is hard for someone with emphysema. But he had been in the hospital once before with a bad cold, and they just pumped him full of antibiotics for a week, and then let him go.

But then the day after he was admitted, my mom called and said he had taken a turn for the worse. So I went to Ohio.

I don't think my dad thought he was going to die, either. The first thing he said when I walked into his room was, "Why did you come?"

17.

2/23/46: For the last two days, I have not only been busy with the purser end of this racket, but also the medical end. The Chief Mate has what I think is a mild pneumonia. Complains of pain in chest and has a temp around 101 and 102. Been pumping the sulfa into him for nearly thirty hours with no apparent results. Something had better break soon.

I went ashore in St. Nazaire last night and found it to be only a hollow shell of a once very fine city. Houses all along the waterfront have been destroyed. Only large piles of bricks remain.

I sprained my ankle badly while jumping from the ship to shore. I thought it was about six feet in the dark, but it must have been ten or twelve. This makes three times I've done this in the last year and a half. I don't think the cartilage and ligaments can stand much more. It takes a lot to make me cry, but I cried myself to sleep last night because the pain was so terrific. Two nembutals had no effect.

18.

When my dad was dying, he saw things. You could tell by the way he kept looking at the air to the right and left of the always-on TV. One day he pointed at the air beside me and said, "That's the man who came to see me." And when I asked, "Who?" he chuckled and waved his hand and said, "Not important."

Another time, when the pulse/oxygen monitor by his bed started beeping the super-loud beep, the beep that summoned the nurse pronto, he opened his eyes wide and looked—not at the nurse and me—but at the air behind us. And he smiled like he was a 15-year-old virgin seeing the most beautiful naked woman on earth, and in a voice that sounded like Louis Armstrong, he said, "Ohhhhh, man."

19.

I am in the doctor's examination room. I am alone with the ultrasound machine. If you've never seen one, an ultrasound machine has the short, squat look of a first grader's desk, only wearing a computer screen and a white plastic sword. It is a first grader's desk, dressed up for Halloween as something from *Star Wars*.

And so I am alone with it, with my pen and paper, and I write the following stuff down. That it is GE model 10 G 10 400 MD. That its System ID number is 212746LOGIc4. That there is a 1-800-GE number on it. That next to the plastic wand is a plastic bottle like the kind you see filled with ketchup at a diner. That the bottle says "Graham-Field Ultrasound Transmission Gel." That said gel, when squirted on one's arm, is blue.

Then this morning's lovely and talented resident physician enters the room, so I put down my pen and assume the position, and we look at the screen.

"I had two on the right side on Monday," I say.

She knows. She waves the wand, up, down, side to side. Ouch.

Onscreen, suddenly, a black hole, which is what follicles look like, in *Star Wars*-Halloween land.

I hear her fingers on the keyboard. Tap, tap. Two small x's appear on either side of the hole.

"How big is it?"

"Seventeen and a half," she says.

"Where's the other one?"

"It must not have matured," she says.

Why does something not mature? The resident could not tell me that. She left the examination room to confer with another doctor, and together they decided to give me my shot, even though the follicle was only at seventeen and a half. And as I was leaning on the examination table, with my pants puddled around my ankles, I studied the ultrasound machine again, and saw that the sword had a condom on it, and inside the condom was the blue jelly, in little waves.

And then I got my shot and even though I asked for a Band-Aid the resident said I didn't need one. So I went home. And when I got there I called the number on the ultrasound. And a woman with a southern accent answered and said, "GE We Care, can I have your System ID number?"

And so I told her the other number I wrote down.

"Can I help you?"

So I told her I wanted to know more about how the sonar works on the ultrasound.

And she said I'd have to talk to the service engineer. And so she transferred me to his extension, and when he answered, I asked him why you have to have a condom full of jelly on the wand when you do the ultrasound. And he said, "because the sound waves have to have a medium to go through," and then he told me to go to the library.

20.

3/3/46: Today is the beginning of the French Mardi Gras which precedes each Lent. The people dress up similar to our kids on Halloween and parade through the streets. I'm afraid this was a rather poor celebration for the French, because of lack of clothes. Most people wore their old civilian issue gas masks for a false face.

21.

I was just inseminated.

Since my insemination, I have done the following things with my body: walked fourteen blocks. Taken the 6 train and then transferred to the E. Stood on the platform and finished reading the *Post*. Drank a small bottle of water. Chewed two pieces of peppermint gum. Offered my *Post* to the smiling man on the train. Walked three more blocks. Bought a latte. Walked home. Walked in the door. Changed my shirt. Washed my face. Peed. Drank more water. Ate a chocolate calcium chew. Masturbated. Ate a handful of animal crackers and some saltines with strawberry jelly. Another chocolate calcium chew. And then sat down here. Chugged the latte.

I am scared of being pregnant now. And I remember sitting in the packed waiting room this morning, the waiting room bursting with cell-phone ringings and high-heel stampings and diamond-ring flashings, and noticing one beleaguered-looking woman who brought her singing two-year-old with her. No, noticing how everyone in the room ignored her. And her child. This was a room, clearly, that did not love children.

Thinking, what is it, exactly, that we want here?

22.

Frank came with me this morning to the insemination. He had to come, ha. He had to come in a sterile plastic container at 8:30 a.m., and then they took his sperm and "washed" it, as they say, to make it more motile, to make it supersperm. It takes them an hour to wash it. So my insemination was scheduled for 9:30 a.m.

And Frank has done this insemination thing before, so he knows the routine. We go there, and they give him the sterile plastic cup, and he writes my name and his name all over it, and then he goes into the collection room, which is basically a closet, only furnished with a VCR, porn magazines, and a chair with a diaper spread across the seat.

And last time I asked him which one he looked at, the magazine or the video, and he said the video. And I asked him what it was called and he said he wasn't sure, he just pressed play and went with it.

So this time I said, you have to get the title for me. And so I was sitting in the waiting room when he came back in and took my pen and paper from me and wrote this down:

VALENTINO'S ASIAN INVASION

And I laughed out loud.

And then he had to go to work, so I sat in the waiting room and drew ladies' feet until it was time to go pick up his supersperm in the test tube. Now here is your quiz: do you know what color washed semen is?

It is pink. Bright pink. And it is thin. It shakes around in the test tube like a tiny sip of diet grapefruit drink.

And I take the test tube (asking the technician again, as I always do, are you sure this is mine, ha ha?), and I swaddle it in my STP motor oil windbreaker, and as I do so, I remember the time I wore this windbreaker on Astor Place and some guy looked at me and said, "STP! Stop Teen Pregnancy!"

And then I go back to the waiting room, and sit awhile longer, until my name is called, my name and another woman's name. Two names at the same time. And we look at each other and smile and follow the resident to the exam rooms. And the woman turns to me right before she goes into her room and says, "We have the same clothes on, did you notice?"

And I look. And it's true. We are both wearing white shirts and black pants.

"It's our lucky outfit," I say.

And then we go through our separate doors, and close them behind us, and as we do I am remembering the psychic I go to see once a year, in January, right after my birthday. I like her for many reasons, one of the foremost being that if you try to go more than once a year, she won't let you. And I asked her then, last January, will I be pregnant? And she said she saw two little heads pop up. And at the time I thought, oh, that's my two

26

children, because Frank and I had decided that was how many we wanted. But then later I thought, maybe it's twins.

And in the exam room I am alone again with my pants off and the ultrasound machine. And I stand there and study the probe. It is naked, without a condom, without jelly. It is very long. It is longer than any penis I have ever, personally, sat on.

And then the resident comes in, this one a blonde in burgundy leather high heels. And I hand her the tiny pink drink and she looks at it and then shows me the names on it and asks, "Is this yours?" And I say, "I hope so, " and climb on the table and assume the position and wince as she puts the speculum in.

Have you ever been inseminated? It is not like laying back on the red velvet divan. It is painful. They use a plunger attached to a long pipette, and they stick the pipette through your cervix, into your uterus, and then they plunge. And if you, like me, have never had any children, then most likely you have never had anything that was not microscopic going into or out of your cervix. Did I mention that the pipette inside your cervix feels like a tiny knife? A tiny knife stabbing you farther inside than you ever knew anything could go?

And you feel the knife stabs for about fifteen seconds, which can seem like quite a long time. And then the resident takes the pipette out and the speculum out and goes away, click, click, there's no place like home.

And I am not supposed to move for fifteen more minutes. "To rest," she said.

23.

3/12/46: I had quite a talk with the Chief Engineer last night, and find him to be a most amazing person. In his spare time, he is a writer of short stories or anecdotes. His mastery of the English language is good, but his style of writing is rather poor, for I have perused a few of his literary attempts. His sense of morals—if such a sense is even present—is sadly wanting. His wife must truly be a very understanding person, and her love for him very deep, because he has been involved in the most scandalous predicaments involving women. He has "wronged" more women—and been caught at it— than are "wronged" in an entire year's publication of *True Confessions* magazine. He is wrapped up in the do- ings of his two sons, both of whom are in their early teens, although his wife is twenty-eight. I can't help liking the fellow, for all his shortcomings.

Fairly heavy seas today. Will soon enter bonus area at the ninth meridian, because of floating mines. Make

$2.50 extra a day, and get an added $10 a month for carrying dangerous cargo.

24.

I wish there were a better word to describe Frank than "husband." "Husband" means we had a nice party one day, where we ate cake, and said words.

Here is what I would like: if there were a word to describe the person who is in your band, the person who stands onstage beside you, in front of the crowd of people, and sings the song you wrote, the song you are too afraid to sing, which is why you are the guitarist. And the song is called "I Love My Mom," and he sings the words like they are not about moms, or love, at all. He sings the words like they are a way to say, "I am going to pinch you."

And so this man, Frank, calls me as he is in the process of trying to find some falafel for lunch. He calls because he wants to tell me what he had forgotten to tell me earlier, that is, the exact scene of the insemination video.

"There was a man," he says, "presumably Valentino. And he was in the process of servicing five women."

"Five women. Was he servicing them with his penis?"

"Yes."

"What about the ones who didn't have access to the penis?"

"They were keeping busy."

"With what?"

"Licking and sucking and stroking, things like that."

"Uh-huh."

He asks me how the insemination was.

"It didn't hurt as much as the last time."

"Because you were used to it," he says.

"No."

"Are you sure it hurt?"

"Yes."

"Are you sure?"

"Yes!"

"You wouldn't like to do it again, at home? Later?"

25.

I felt more beautiful during the six weeks my dad was in the hospital than in any time in recent memory.

It is unsettling to admit this. It feels shameful. Like how dare it happen, how dare anything beautiful happen, anything related to beauty, when a person you love is dying.

And as it was happening I felt it, and asked myself why, and decided it was because I was so focused on my dad that I began to reflect him. And my dad, when he was dying, was a very beautiful man.

And it is so wonderful to be beautiful. It is so wonderful to be beautiful as you chase the respiratory specialist down the hall, the sixty-year-old respiratory specialist with the bedside manner of a parking meter, and yell his name, and make him turn around. And to stand in front of the respiratory specialist and say, "Please explain to me again my dad's prognosis." And to see the respiratory specialist, who is bald but for white tufts over each ear, stroke his chin with his hand, and look at your breasts, which are encased in a bright red and pink bra, which is showing slightly through your white T-shirt, and you know this, but you can't help it, because you thought you were only coming here for the weekend, and so you brought one bra, and one pair of khakis and two of the same white T-shirts, and you have been wearing them now, for three weeks straight.

And it is wonderful to feel your breasts, in the red and pink bra, hardening under the gaze of the respiratory specialist, and to feel like it would be entirely appropriate for you and the respiratory specialist, who is old enough to be your father, to lay down, right here, in the hall, and do it, as the plump nurses troll by with their plastic buckets of drugs like so many posies, because you are together, you and the respiratory specialist, in your nothing you can do.

And that is part of how I felt more beautiful than anytime in recent memory, but that isn't the whole of it. That's more sex-beauty.

The beauty-beauty part came when I drove the car alone to the hospital, because my mom was taking a day off. When I drove sixty miles an hour down Chagrin Boulevard with all the windows open, and sang that old Replacements song, "Rattlesnake."

No, that isn't it either. That was more fake-beauty, like when you look like you always look, but you act like you're in a music video.

This is embarrassing. Maybe I wasn't beautiful at all. My dad was beautiful, though.

On the last day of his life, he had some moments where he was completely lucid and others where he was totally out of it.

So when he looked up at me from the bed and said, "I soiled my pants," I couldn't tell if he was confused or not. My dad had never said those words to me before. My dad had never soiled his pants, to my knowledge. He had had catheters.

I was opening a package of chocolate pudding, to feed him. I was looking for the plastic spoon. I did not understand. I was opening pudding. I was beautiful. I was an idiot.

"Do you want them changed?" I asked.

This was one of our last conversations on earth, you understand.

"Yes," he said, looking at me like, of course, you imbecile.

26.

3/16/46: Today the last of the coal has been unloaded and we are sailing tomorrow at 0700.

The very last day that I am here, we would run into a perfect Luger. The guy wanted 18,000 francs for it, and I didn't have it. Somehow the Steward bought it, but I don't know for what. I will try to work on him to get the gun if it is at all possible. I can't figure out why I go so hog wild when I see a gun. Perhaps it is the feeling of superiority it gives a person.

27.

Last night I took myself and my possible embryo over to Madison Square Garden to hear AC/DC.

I love AC/DC. The first electric guitar I ever bought was a Gibson SG, and I chose it because that's the kind AC/DC's lead guitarist, Angus Young, plays.

And even now, when I play guitar at home, I have three songs I like to play over and over. One is "I Love My Mom." You know that one already. The others are "Six Pack" by Black Flag, and "Hell's Bells" by AC/DC, both of which I sing really girly and slow. But when I am singing them girly and slow I am thinking, and loving, the way they are sung in the original, hard and fast and all boy, boy, boy. It's like my girly singing is my way of loving their boyishness. Because I can't be a boy, no matter how much I love them. Love boys.

Frank was tired, and didn't want to come with me.

And now we live only six blocks from the Garden, so the luxury of being able to walk down the street and see AC/DC on a whim is new. But of course you cannot see AC/DC on a whim, I discovered, because their shows sell out. This show sold out three weeks ago, the woman at the Garden ticket window told me.

And I have never bought a ticket from a scalper before, but I remembered this young couple I had just passed on Eighth Avenue and 33rd, who had been holding their tickets very conspicuously. So I left the ticket window and went back to see if they were still there. They were. And when I asked them if they were selling their ticket, the guy explained that they were waiting for someone, but he wasn't showing up. And if he didn't show up in five more minutes, they would let me have the ticket.

So I waited for five minutes, and then the guy gave me the ticket. For free.

And I stood there like ack, ack, I was so flabbergasted.

And then, as they were walking away, the guy looked over his shoulder and said the seat should be pretty good, because the ticket was from "the band."

That's what he called AC/DC: "the band."

And then I sprinted into the Garden, scared it was some kind of joke, scared the ticket was fake, illegal, something young couples give away nowadays, just for cruel fun. And I thrust the ticket at one of the guys in the green polyester blazers, and waited for the alarms to go off. But they didn't go off and didn't go off as I followed him down the steps, feeling like a ball in a pinball machine, headed to a pocket where there would be a super-high, light-flashing, bell-ringing score. And finally I came to the folding chair that the ticket had turned into. And I was standing a mere five rows away from where Angus Young was already sweating a river in his red velvet schoolboy uniform.

And did I say this already? That music is the best theater? That it's so ridiculous it doesn't even make any sense? That there should be these people onstage, standing there, wiggling little strings on blocks of wood slung around their necks? Jumping up and down and wiggling the strings? Jumping up and down and hopping back and forth and dancing on tippy-toes, wiggling strings? And how if you were deaf, and just saw them doing that, you would think, what the hell? What is that? And if you were never on earth before and someone had to explain it to you they would have to say there's this thing called music, and it's invisible. And it floats around in the air and it fills up whole rooms, and more than rooms, whole homes, whole football fields, whole stadiums. And we know it is there, because we can hear it through these little holes on either sides of our heads. And if we turn it up really loud we can feel it, we can feel it in our bodies, vibrating. But we can't see it. The only thing we can see is people jumping and wiggling.

And that's the thing right there, that makes me believe in everything that makes no sense. When Angus Young plays the opening chords to "Hell's Bells," we know that something is here in the Garden that wasn't here before, something huge and inexplicable, and it is not the giant, papier-mache bell that drops from the ceiling. It is a presence, and even though it seems to be associated with Angus Young, it is not Angus Young.

And it is like a joke, almost, that we only have Angus Young to look at, Angus Young who is forty-five now, for god's sake, in his schoolboy outfit and his wedding ring, when we hear this gargantuan thing arriving, this giant presence, this god. It is a joke that we can't see it, that we see only this shadow, this Angus Young fidgeting in his red velvet shorts, when we know as sure as we are standing here that a freaking king has come.

28.

My brother and I are not very close. I already told you that. So I was surprised and happy when I opened the mail and found he had sent me a guest pass to meet him at this oceanographic conference in Providence, where he has to go on business.

The conference is September 11-14. September 13 is my brother's birthday. So I want to go to the conference to see my brother on his birthday. And I want to learn something about sonar in one of the conference tutorials. And I want to talk to my brother about his kids.

I want to do all this, but I am scared of stepping on my brother's toes.

I am scared of my brother, a little.

29.

I spent an hour today trying to stuff my dad's hair into my new locket. I ended up using a pair of tweezers. The problem was that he didn't have that much hair, and then the lock I cut was not very long. I wanted to cut the long lock, the piece that he brushed back from the center of his forehead, but I was afraid that if I did that his hair would look stupid in the coffin. So I took a short hunk from the back, about an inch.

I took the lock of hair right after he died. Moments after. I was surprised I had the wherewithal to cut his hair at all, but I had been thinking about it for a while, that if he died, I wanted that. And there weren't any scissors around, so I did it with my army knife. Which he had given me.

And so I have this hunk of hair that I have kept in a plastic bag. And yesterday, my friend Liz was in town from Boston and her mom died in November, and she was looking for a locket, too, to put a few of her mom's rosary beads in. So I decided we might as well go up to Tiffany's. I had never been there before, but I figured it's so big, it's such an institution, it will be open late on a Saturday night. But it closes at six. So we got there at six minutes to six, and took the delightful wood-paneled elevator up to the second-floor silver-jewelry department, and found these plain lockets like little silver eggs, and we bought them.

Liz left this morning. And then this afternoon I took out the hair. And I don't remember tying it at all, but I did, with one of those paper-covered wires you find around bags of sandwich bread. And I sniffed the hair but it didn't smell like my dad. And I took a bit out, and maybe it was because my dad had been in the hospital for six weeks without having a real hot-water shampoo, but the hair just didn't want to curl up in the egg. I would get a few hairs in, and then they would pop out. And it's late summer now so I had the windows open and a breeze came through and some of the hairs blew around, and I just got mad, like my dad was a cat I was trying to get in the carrier, and he wouldn't go.

30.

My dad tried to tell me, when I was twelve, about the importance of everyday actions. How everyday actions make up your life. He was sitting at his desk, the one where he wrote the checks with a machine that embossed the amounts into the paper.

"Everyday," he said, "you're writing the record."

He repeated this several times. And each time he said it he pantomimed it: moving his arm from left to right, wiggling his empty fingers.

31.

3/18/46: Today a large sea hawk lighted on our mizzenmast and chased away all the sea gulls. The Captain allowed the Third Mate and I to take shots at it with our pea shooters. I couldn't hit the thing with my .25 because the ship was pitching so much. Finally, he broke out one of the ship's new .38s and let me fire that. Still couldn't do much. If he's still around when the weather gets calmer we are going to take another try at it. Sure was fun while it lasted.

32.

The older I get the more profound that song "Row, Row, Row Your Boat" seems. Especially the fact that it is sung in rounds. When I hear those last few people still singing when everyone else has fallen silent, it gives me shivers.

On my dad's last day, he had this gurgling sound in his chest. He had had fluid-y sounds before, but this was more pronounced. The nurse came in and suctioned him, but it didn't seem to make any difference.

My dad looked a little scared. His eyes were darting around. Or maybe that was normal. Anyway, I was scared. I sat beside him and held his hand. And he started doing this thing he had learned in Breathing Class, which is what he called the special exercise class he went to, for people with heart and lung problems. The thing was pursed-lip exhaling, and it is the exact same kind of breathing you see women do when they are in labor.

And the sight of my dad, doing those exhales, as his lungs were making the gurgling sound, was like watching my ship go down, my ship with my captain on it.

Watching all this because, for whatever reason, I was not on the same ship my dad was on. I was on the ship where I sat next to him, and held his hand, and heard a sound in my head like a plane taking off.

33.

There is this funny two-week period of time after the insem-ination, before you take the pregnancy test, where you are just left on your own. No ultrasounds, nothing.

And so I sit in the bedroom, and eat graham crackers, and look out the window. And in between all the apartment buildings, I can see this thing in the air that looks like a whale's tail, only painted red, white, and blue. And it is the giant, rising-up fin of the cruise ship that is docked in the

Hudson and leaves late every Sunday afternoon. And I love to see it out there, it is like seeing my pet tin whale. And so I sit there and smile at it, and let myself think I am pregnant.

I let myself think I am pregnant, but really, I want proof. And so I listen to myself. And I hear nothing. Nothing much. And I remember how my regular, non-fertility doctor told me that when you are pregnant, your organs change place in your body.

"It's like science fiction," she said. She was giggling.

And I imagine my organs floating around freely inside me, as if they were underwater.

Organs need air going through them, to make sound. Otherwise we can't hear them. My friend Patrick fixes organs in churches all over Manhattan. My friend Patrick stands fifty feet up, adjusting an organ's primary valve. He does this even during funerals. Only then, he does it very quietly.

34.

My brother is sending me e-mail about the conference:

"I avoid the tutorials like the plague. They're usually a bunch of PhDs talking algorithms to one another.

I am normally tied to the booth glad-handing. A lot depends on who is in from the UK, though. Have fun. Love,"

My plan is to take the train up, then go to an afternoon tutorial called "Environmental Acoustics I: Models and Simulations." After that I figure we will celebrate my brother's birthday. There is a big event in Providence that night where they light fires on the water.

35.

3/20/46: Today has been beautiful out. This morning it was rather rough, but this afternoon it calmed down. I don't think a man could find more peace and contentment than out here at sea. The ship rolls gently from sunrise to sunset.

The Second Mate has a touch of pleurisy, but his temperature is not high enough to warrant sulfa. The Chief Cook laid open his scalp and I had to shave him bald as a "Q" on top to get at it.

I was on a bike this morning, pedaling. This was a bike with the Internet attached to it. So I asked the Internet, "Am I pregnant?" And I got a list of Web sites about prenatal health and maternity clothes.

So I went onto one of the health Web sites. It had a "What to Expect" column for when you are one, two, three, etc., weeks pregnant. And even though I was inseminated only seven days ago, I would be in my third week of pregnancy, since they start counting from the beginning of your cycle.

And in my third week of pregnancy, this site said, I should expect to have some spotting, from when the fertilized egg implants itself in the uterine wall. And then the site explained what the fertilized egg looks like now: a fluid-filled sac that is busy dividing, and will keep dividing, until eventually, it splits into two parts; the part that becomes the placenta, and the part that becomes the baby.

After that I went home because I had told my friend Patrick that I would be there in case he needed to call me because his wife's operation went horribly wrong. His wife has this condition where her eggs start dividing all by themselves, without being fertilized. They do this while they are just sitting on her ovaries. And after a while all this stuff accumulates on her ovaries, stuff the size of softballs. And the crazy thing is, this stuff is not just stuff. It has hair in it, sometimes. And teeth.

This is the third time Patrick's wife has undergone this procedure. They go through a hole under her belly button, and dig the stuff out.

Patrick called around noon. "She's OK," he said.

We talked about what a crazy thing it was.

And Patrick told me a story about one lady with this condition, who had also had thyroid cancer. And when they dug her stuff out, they found that the stuff also had thyroid tissue in it, and that the thyroid tissue was also cancerous.

I was trying to think of the right botanical analogy.

"It's like a spore," I said, but I didn't think that was right.

"It's like an internal twin," said Patrick.

I am walking down the street to the dry cleaner, with my black pants balled up in my arms.

And this is Ninth Avenue I am walking down, and let me tell you, my friend, there is a lot going on, on Ninth Avenue. There are men in white T-shirts, standing around. Cigarettes in their hands. Cigarettes in their mouths.

I look at people now, smoking. Lately I have been trying to think of illnesses in terms of metaphor. I said illnesses but I mean behaviors.

What does it mean that someone thinks they need a cigarette many times a day? What does it mean to need fire like that? Fire all the time?

Does it mean you are too watery? Does it mean you feel you have no spark?

Does it mean you have a need to see your breath? That it's not enough to hear it, to feel it? You need to see the image? You need to see the smoke?

My dad smoked Kools. Since he was twelve, he smoked. He quit in his fifties.

That is why he had emphysema. That is why he died, basically.

My dad is dead. And as I type this, by the window, on the rainy day, I am alive, yes. I am living. But sometimes it doesn't feel like I am doing it fast enough, or hard enough, or all the way. And it is times like that when I can understand wanting a cigarette in my hand, then my mouth, then my hand again. Holding the cigarette. Tending to the cigarette. Giving the cigarette what it needs. Tapping it in the ashtray. Sucking on it.

Then flicking it in the street, like it meant nothing to me.

38.

I remember telling my dad, when he was dying, that I was going to be pregnant soon. I could feel him getting ready to leave, and I wanted to give him a reason to stay. He knew we were trying to have a kid, and even though he didn't say much about it, every once in a while he would ask me, "Are you pregnant yet?" and I knew he was excited.

And sometimes I would sit in the hospital room with him, and think that this was my job, at this stage in my life: to get this new life form into my body. And it seemed hard enough, given my circumstances.

But then it seemed like a cakewalk compared to his job, which was to get his life force out. And when I thought about this, I would look down at the air in front of my stomach, and think about how it would feel to know I had to propel myself out there. And it seemed impossible.

But of course, no one really has to do that work themselves. The body helps. The body kicks you out. Or maybe, it's not the body kicking you out at all. Maybe it's space, inviting you in.

39.

3/12/46: I saw my first real good case of shock the other day. Man fell into the water between the ship and the dock while the wind was blowing the ship against the dock. Suffered only contusions to the knee but was really out. I knew what to do, but wasn't very efficient about it. I was going to give adrenaline, but didn't think he warranted it. Brought him out of it by soaking blankets in hot water.

40.

I am standing in front of the refrigerator, with the door open, eating. I am sticking the spoon with the creamy peanut butter on it into the jar of strawberry jelly. I do not want any bread. I do not want to sit down. I am hot and sweaty and possibly pregnant and I want to stand in front of the refrigerator and stuff things in my mouth.

If there are songs for every conceivable type of work, if there are sea shanties, why aren't there labor songs?

I close the refrigerator door, put the dirty spoon in the sink, walk to the bed, and lie down on it.

Tomorrow, I decide, I am going to eat lobster. And corn.

41.

3/23/46: Today we rigged up a fishing line off the side of the ship. Use no bait but a white rag. I think the ship is moving too fast to catch any fish. Tomorrow we will pass the tip of Florida and go through a place called the "hole in the wall." This will require us to slow down, so the fishing ought to be pretty good.

3/24/46: We dragged in the fishing line without catching any fish. The speed of the ship is too great for fishing. It is fun to watch the flying fish. They are about six inches long and skim over the water like small birds for a hundred feet or so.

Water here is shark infested.

42.

I do not think I am pregnant anymore.

I am not sure why. I just don't. I was feeling all fertile and blossoming there for a second. And now I just feel like me, on earth. I was floating a little bit there before. I was like a very small version of a Macy's Thanksgiving Day Parade balloon. I was puffy and needed handlers. I was lumbering through the air, a couple inches off the ground. I was veering toward lampposts.

Now I am just here, sitting on my ass. Drinking coffee and not getting off.

I took the early detection pregnancy test this morning, and it was negative. I am feeling negative. Of course I am even taking the early detection test too early. You are supposed to be able to take it three days before your period is due. My period isn't due for seven days.

I am trying to think about sound now because my friend Yelena asked me to be the sound designer for this play she's directing. It's *Scenes from an Execution* by Howard Barker. I read it yesterday. It's about a woman named Galactia who has gotten a commission from the city of Venice to do a painting of the Battle of Lepanto, which is this major Venetian sea battle. The play is kind of high drama. The opening scene has Galactia ranting about how dead men float with their asses in the air.

I met Yelena because I was an actor in another play she did. I did it as an experiment, to see if I liked acting. And I learned that I like acting OK.

And I was pleased and surprised that Yelena asked me to be her sound designer, since I have never sound-designed a play before. So Yelena and I met last night to talk about sound, but instead we ended up talking about what we've been reading lately. And she said that she's been reading this Russian writer named Alexander Vvedensky. And she explained that Vvedensky has this idea that time, space, objects, and movement are much more fluid than we think. And he says that moments happen all the time when time blends into space, and space blends into objects, and objects into movement, etc. And when these moments happen, he calls it "shimmering."

And Vvedensky uses this great image, Yelena said, to talk about time and why our ideas about time prevent us from seeing it as it really is. And the image is of a mouse, walking across a field. And he said the way we think about time, we see the mouse moving forward in a straight line. But if we stopped thinking about time as a linear progression, we would instead see the mouse stepping. And we would see every step, and every step would be a new step.

And that made me think, I have been numbering all these writings. But if I take into account what Vvedensky is saying, I realize that all I am doing is trying to make this writing reflective of a linear concept of time. If I were to embrace his idea, I would be numbering each of these passages "1."

1.

We have no curtains in our apartment yet. So Frank and I are naked and making love in front of our windows, our windows surrounded by other windows, our windows facing even more windows.

And I imagine the whole city, making love and sweating, a celebration.

It is Labor Day Eve.

I want a ficus tree, dripping with sweat.

I want children knocking at the door, singing work songs.

1.

Labor Day in the garment district starts as usual, at seven a.m., with the sound of the sewing machines shrugging their tin shoulders.

My gym is closed. After Frank leaves, I put on my sneakers and jog around our apartment for twenty-nine minutes. I jog in a circle around our bed, then go out of our bedroom into the living room, where I make another circle around the pile of boxes. Then I go back. After a while I get kind of dopey in my jogging and bang my hand into the door.

I jog with my knuckle bleeding. I jog in circles, in silence, just the sewing machines and my raggedy breath.

1.

Imagine a hundred million pieces of paper, each piece with the words DAD DAD DAD DAD written all over it. Paper stacked twenty-five feet in the air. Paper so high I would have to keep it outside, and surround it with a fence. Paper like my pet giraffe, in Hell's Kitchen.

The urge is to write my dad into existence. To sit here, and do an incantation. I believe in Mary Worth. I believe in my dead dad.

I just called my mom. My mom is not my dad. My mom is my mom.

I asked my mom the last time I was home, two weeks after the funeral, if she had heard from my dad. I meant, in a dream or something. She said no. Flat. My mom doesn't like to think about things like that.

But then as I was sitting there, across the kitchen table from her, she suddenly put one hand over her eye. And I asked, "Why are you doing that?" And she said, "Because something's wrong with my eye." And I asked, "What?" And she said, "I keep seeing this light."

And I said, "Describe it." And she said, "It's like these neon bars, in a semi-circle." And then she took her hand off her eye and put it over her other one.

"I see it with both eyes," she said.

Then she put her hands in her lap and looked at the clock on the wall.

"I see it wherever I look," she said.

And then she stood up and went to lie down on her bed with her eyes closed.

1.

5/11/46: Each night about 6 to 8, I sit on the bridge and shoot the bull with the Chief Mate. He is interesting to talk to, but we usually wind up talking about his girl. I met her in Mobile, and she is really something to talk about. He plans to get married and settle down ashore, but he doesn't know just what he wants to do. He is bright and catches on easily, so he shouldn't have too much trouble. A fellow his age—twenty-one—has a great advantage in that he can sit for his Masters papers and be sailing as a captain in a few years. He would be about the youngest Master in the seas if he did.

We may have a little trouble in Italy since we will get there just about election time. From what I hear, these elections are not always peaceful affairs.

1.

Call-and-response is my favorite song form on earth. It doesn't matter what the words are. It just has to be one voice calling, and then many voices responding, and then one voice calling again, and then many voices responding again. I hear that and I almost always start crying immediately. I am not sure why, except that I feel like I have done the call part so many times, both literally and metaphorically, without hearing any reply, that call-and-response is like an aural fantasy for me, a place where no pleas go unanswered, where no questions go unheard. Call-and-response is what I wish prayer were.

I went to see the sea shanties at the South Street Seaport Museum last night. Sea shanties, as you probably know, originated as work songs. They were meant to assist the sailors in hauling and heaving; they also served to quickly bond a group of sailors who had never worked together before.

And last night's sea shanties were supposed to be performed on *The Peking*, the museum's fully restored, 1911 merchant vessel, but *The Peking* was booked for some kind of party, so the shanties were sung in the Melville Gallery, a storefront space on Water Street.

The group singing the shanties was called the New York Packet. They were a loose collection of about twelve people, with some drifting in and out as the evening wore on. A couple members had guitars, and one had a banjo, but mostly the tunes were sung without accompaniment. People in the group would take turns being the caller. It was the caller's decision what song to do.

One guy stood out. He was the oldest in the group, maybe late sixties. He was in good shape for his age, with powerful arms and his shirt tucked in. He was losing his hair on top, but what was there was long and pulled back in a silver braid. Frank, they called him.

And Frank had that thing I love, which is that freaky enthusiasm that makes people gorgeous at the same time they are acting a little strange. Frank clearly loved singing sea shanties, and was one of the only ones in the group who would pantomime pulling the ropes as he was singing, "Heave away, haul away." He was also the only one who would yell out these little cries, these joyous war-whoops, between verses, that maybe no real seaman ever yelled, I don't know, but it didn't feel that way. It felt like a real seaman on a boat in the middle of the ocean would make that sound, hell yes.

He reminded me of this thing I read once, in a women's magazine. It was an advice column, and a young woman had written in saying she was embarrassed to have an orgasm with her guy because whenever she came, she crossed her eyes. And I remember reading that, and thinking, oh my god. Because I have seen those ancient art images from Asia and India, of gods and goddesses with crossed eyes. And I knew, too, that Kabuki actors crossed their eyes at climactic moments. And it seemed to me that this woman's spontaneous eye-crossing was the evidence-of-god equivalent of the shadow of the Virgin Mary appearing on the side of someone's barn.

And the thing I love about the Franks of the world is that when a god shows up like that, in the urge to make a seemingly inexplicable gesture, they don't fight it. They just surrender. And if they feel self-conscious and ashamed, they don't pay it any mind.

And it is such a privilege to be around people like that, because they can show you things. Like when Frank was singing, and he had his eyes closed, and his mouth open, I swear, I could see his death-face in his living one. I could see him lying back in the bed, with his big, beautiful, gray head pointing at the ceiling, and his spirit flying out of his mouth, and nothing we could do about it.

1.

5/15/46: The Chief Engineer got us laughing like mad tonight at supper by telling us a tale that happened in Yokohama, on the trip before I joined this ship. It seems that over there, there was a big Negro private in the US army who had charge of 200 Japs unloading ships. It so happened that they were unloading trucks at the time of this incident and the entire crew of the ship was standing around the rail watching. As the Japs were heaving the trunks down the ramp, the Negro private would cry out to them in a loud voice, "Blow your tops!" The next instant two hundred Japs would reply in one voice, "Bullshit!" This kept the crew laughing for hours until the Mate took aside one of the Japs and coached him in a reply. So when the Negro got the words out for another yell, a small voice piped up before the others and replied, "Blow it out your own!"

1.

Last night was the first meeting for Yelena's play. We met at her apartment. And we went around the table, and everyone talked about what they had been thinking about lately, as far as *Scenes from an Execution* goes.

And when my turn came, I told them about seeing the sea shanties, and how great they were. And then everyone was talking about the sea-battle painting in the play, and the problem of how we were going to represent a painting that is repeatedly referred to as this incredible work of art that causes people to collapse, sobbing.

My assignment is to figure out what kind of sound a painting like this would make. So far I have no ideas.

1.

My artist-friend Jerry from Boston just called. I haven't heard from him in over a month. And he told me about this thing he has been making out of aluminum drawers from an old wool factory.

It is a nine-foot ocean liner on wheels. He said the idea came because he and all these other artists in his building are fighting to keep from being evicted from their studios. And

Jerry said he was having this moment of despair, thinking that they would never win the fight, and he would have to be out of his studio in a few months. And he was freaking out thinking how he would never get all his stuff out of his studio, because Jerry is basically a flea-market-aholic. And so the boat idea came, he said, and he started making it out of the drawers, and then filling the drawers with these other things he has, these steel shapes that were originally used as patterns to cut appliques for children's clothing. He bought all the patterns, and then a ton of the sample appliques, in one fell swoop, from a guy at the Thunderbird Flea Market in Miami.

And so I asked him what images the patterns were of, and he said, "Every image you can think of."

And I asked, "Every apple? Every snail?"

And he said, "Every apple, every snail, every flower, everything. Hundreds of forms."

And so Jerry is building this ship of metal drawers with all the steel patterns lying in them quietly, like the letters of a dead alphabet. And all around the top and outside of the boat he has sewn the felt appliques onto little flags, so the boat has eighty flags now. And the boat is sitting in his studio like that, on wheels, ready to go, as he is fighting to stay.

He is calling the boat *The Thunderbird*.

"I don't know what the hell it is," he said.

1.

5/24/46: Today we passed through the Strait of Gibraltar into the Mediterranean. This is a busy channel, for we must have seen three dozen ships during the course of the day. The Rock of Gibraltar was not as pictured by Prudential Life Insurance Company. The Rock has immense concrete slabbing on the west side and is pockmarked with holes for guns. We were flashed by blinker lights from there to give our destination and the name of our ship.

I have been practicing using a sextant each night. I can use one pretty accurately now. Only those stars are used that come out earliest at night, such as Jupiter, Arcturus, and Venus. I still have trouble recognizing these stars early, but when all the stars are out and the constellations are found, it is easy.

1.

I love my brother. I love my brother, even though I feel like he is going to beat me up when I ask him about his children. Even when I imagine myself doing it in the gentlest way possible. I still see him just standing up, at the birthday restaurant, and punching my lights out.

Why do I think this? Has my brother ever once, ever in my whole life, beaten me up?

No. We weren't even close enough for that.

And as I am writing this I am also thinking, what's the big deal? So he gave up his kids. He must have felt he couldn't take care of them. Why is that bad? Isn't that the right thing to do, the responsible thing, rather than try to raise them when you feel you can't?

Yes. I would think so. But that was before this new problem came up, this problem of I am going to die, and I want children, and I can't seem to have them.

And I don't even want to say this, but this morning was the morning that, according to the doctor, I was supposed to take the home pregnancy test. But I have been taking the early detection tests all week, and they always say no, and when I got up this morning, I felt tired and cranky and thought, I can't do it.

1.

5/29/46: Genova, as the Dagoes spell it, is sure some town. The place has not been touched much by bombs, and the stores have just about as much as we do.

When we entered the harbor, we had to shoot the fire hoses on the people to keep them off the ship. They will break their necks to get a hold of American cigarettes and candy. One carton of cigarettes will bring $7 in American money and you can get anything in cameras, binoculars, and guns.

There are no American soldiers here in the city. Most of them are in Trieste. They will be in the city this weekend for the election, which will be a big affair. There are three parties—the Communists, Republicans, and the Monarchists. Which will win is hard to say.

We are anchored next to an American ship that was mined on her maiden trip in '43 and jackknifed in the middle.

Remembered now that today is my birthday.

1.

I have a cold. I can't speak or hear well. It is sort of fun.

The locksmith is here, putting new locks on our doors. His name is Dror. I thought it was something I was mis-hearing so I made him spell it out, and then as he was saying the letters I wrote them down, and then I held up the paper with the letters on it, so he could see them.

"Yes," he said. "Dror."

And now Dror is around the corner from my desk, drilling into the door frame. I can't see him but I can hear him.

Maybe this is something I can use for the play.

1.

Today I signed up for the high-end fertility doctor's class on how to give yourself shots. I guess "shots" is an old term; the doctor called them "injectables."

"Injectables often work when clomiphene hasn't," he said, and then told me the downside, which is that the odds for multiple births increase: fifteen to twenty percent for twins; five percent for triplets.

I will be injecting drugs from the Pergonal family, he said.

I smiled when I heard that. That the drugs have a family.

1.

6/8/46: I have seen many things in Genoa, the best being the Cemetery of Stalingo.

The prostitutes here outnumber the rest of the population. They are vulgar on the street beyond description, but they seem to thrive, since I have two GC cases now. Can't do much with them, since they continue to patronize these women.

Took part in a gun fray during the election here. Didn't hit anyone but sure used the ammunition. Everyone packs a rod here and there are gun fights every night. Republicans won the election.

1.

I am overtired. I got back from Providence at two a.m. I still have my cold. I can't sleep because Frank is on a business trip and we are in this new apartment and I am not used to the noises and I think there are prowlers. So at night when I am supposed to be sleeping I am busy lying down and then getting up and running into the kitchen with the boxcutter. The boxcutter is our home security system because my dad willed me one of his guns, the one he had to wait two years to get, the Seacamp, but I am afraid to take it.

1.

8/20/46: Quite a time has lapsed since I last wrote in this book. The rest of the return voyage from Italy was fraught with dissension—both between the crew and passengers. A large outbreak of fighting broke before we hit Cuba resulting in a cut face for the Steward. There was entirely too much drinking on everyone's part.

The Captain was under the weather most of the time. The crew was going to make all kinds of charges against everyone, but nothing came of it. We spent a week in Cuba, which is a beautiful country, then sailed for New Orleans. The hottest weather I ever experienced in my life was in New Orleans. You couldn't move without sweating.

I'm now on my way to Germany. We just passed the Tortugas at seven p.m. tonight. I'm the only one left of the old crew of officers. I sure hated to see Freddy Hoeske go, for he was my best buddy.

We have on board 8,000 tons of flour for Bremen. It is the start of a new voyage with new experiences. I sure have seen a hell of a lot of Europe in the last few months and still more is coming.

My dad was twenty-two when he wrote that.

1.

My brother turned forty-four last night. "Four is a bad number for me," he said. "But I guess I couldn't stay forty-three forever."

And I remember my father saying, a week before he died, "Well, it looks like this is about the end of the road."

And I want to kick myself every time I think of this, that instead of comforting him, I asked, "Is that OK?"

He said, "Well, there's not much I can do about it."

1.

5/30/46: Tonight, the Steward—since we saw him unload 1,500 bars of soap to sell—took us up to a place called Cappura as a treat on him to sort of salve us up. This is a beautiful nightclub and restaurant located on the side of the Alps. It is a building thirty stories high and looks over all of Genoa. From the atmosphere of the place, you would have never known there had been a war, for there was an orchestra there, and the food was excellent. I had a steak, which is almost impossible to get in this country. The entire place is enclosed in glass and overlooks the bay. It was beautiful.

1.

Finally, when it was actually happening, when the nurse showed us the signs of pulmonary failure, the blood pooling at the knees, the lowered pulse, I still wasn't sure. We had already been down that road before, with the nurses saying he would be gone in a day. And then of course, he was still there two weeks later.

So I didn't know what to think as my mom and I were sitting there, on either side of him, hearing the terrifying bubbly breathing, the terrifying bubbly breathing that seemed worse than any before, and that was not stopping, even after suction, and that was so scary I was kind of tuning it out. And so it was my mom who noticed he was taking a long time between breaths. And then it was like Jesus Christ. And each of us were already holding a hand. And so we leaned in together, and took turns, like a song, and said,

"Love you so much."

"Such a good man."

"Such a good dad."

"Such a good buddy."

"Love you."

"Love you."

"Love you."

"Love you," like sirens, only from Ohio. Like fat-cheeked sirens. As he passed between us, with his eyes closed.

1.

Yesterday, I went up to Providence on the train. I went up on the route the train takes, by the water, past all the marinas with the sailboats bobbing in them. And I walked into the Providence Convention Center, into the exhibition hall, and found my brother in a booth, standing beside some sonar equipment, under a bouquet of "Happy Birthday" balloons. And he was busy, so he gave me his badge and I went to my

"Environmental Acoustics I: Models and Simulations" tutorial, where three PhDs were supposed to be presenting papers. And the first was "Challenges in Environmental Acoustics" by Paul C. Etter, and the minute Paul C. Etter started talking I knew I was in over my head, and I just wrote down the phrases I understood. And one of the first things I wrote down was "environment is a function of death." And it was only because Paul C. Etter used transparencies—his whole talk was basically him reciting the words on about 400 transparencies—that I saw that he had actually said, "depth," not "death."

Then I sat through the second paper, which was "Characterization of Coastal Environments for Acoustic Models," by Michael Incz, who also used transparencies, only his were fancier, with colored graphs. One in particular I admired had a scattering of bright pink and orange dots. It was titled "Sound/Speed vs. Time/Distance."

And after him was the last paper, the one with the fabulous title: "Simulating an Autonomous Oceanographic Sampling Network: A Multi-Fidelity Approach to Simulating Systems of Systems" by Drs. Roy and Elise Turner, who were experts in artificial intelligence, and who, it turned out, had failed to show up.

And so after the Turners non-appearance I went back to see my brother and he gave me the key to his hotel room and I sat there for a while staring out the window at the water, which was not the ocean but a little man-made, concrete pond attached to a little man-made, concrete river. And the residents of Providence were starting to gather around this water for the evening's Waterfire event. And by the time my brother came and got me for dinner, there were five camp-fires somehow burning in the pond, and two ribbon-hatted gondoliers circling them in golden gondolas. And my brother and I found that by pressing our ears to the unopen-able hotel room window we could hear some low thrum-mings, thrummings which made us think that the event called Waterfire might be accompanied by the music known as Classic Rock. And then my brother said he would rather be beaten to death than go to Firewater. He called it that. So we went to find dinner.

And of course every restaurant was busy "because of Water-fire," the hostesses said, nodding forward slightly, with long shiny blond hair, nodding and smiling like very nice horses, but at last we found a place, some Napa Valley place with pictures of grapes on the menu.

And so we sat across the table from each other, birthday brother and sister, and dipped the bread in green oil, And then I gave my brother a Sting CD, and asked about his kids. And my brother did not clock me. Instead he sighed and told me what I pretty much already knew but had forgotten, or maybe just needed to hear again, which was that he was in his twenties then, and really fucked up, and didn't think twice, knew he couldn't handle it. Could barely take care of himself, knew he couldn't handle parenting. And his gal agreed. And then he said, "And that was sixteen years ago, this Saturday."

And then I got it: birthday. The twins we don't know have a birthday.

My brother and I walked to the Providence train station.

1.

I am pregnant now. I got pregnant without any drugs. Freestyle. I had been taking a break —procrastinating, really— before starting the shots.

I think I got pregnant because of the play. It scrambled my brain that much.

Despite the fact that I was the sound engineer, I was onstage for the entire play. I sat at a table in the back with Patrick, who I had roped into helping me, and we made the sound for the painting, which ended up involving a broken record player, a music box, and a party horn. And as part of being onstage, I sometimes had lines, from the script, to say.

One of these lines was the reponse part of what I would describe as a call-and-response exchange with Galactia. She was making an impassioned speech about the difficulties of depicting the sailors' deaths in her painting, and at certain points I was supposed to interject the words, "The dying! The dying!"

And I discovered that I could not stand there, in my sound-designer non-costume costume of T-shirt and jeans, and say "The dying! The dying!" and have it seem anything but ridiculous.

And so I tried to think of what else I could say. Something that would mean "The dying! The dying!" but in my own words.

And so I asked Yelena, the director, if I could say, "I love you," instead.

And then every night when I said it, I tried to say it so it meant, "This is intolerable."

1.

There was an intermission in the play. During it, I liked to stand backstage with Oleg and Dima. Oleg and Dima are two Russian brothers who are eighteen and twenty years old.

When I first met them, I thought they were twins. They are both thin and blond, with light eyes and pale skin. But after a while I saw the difference: Oleg's nose is more like a button. Dima's hair is thicker.

Oleg and Dima were playing two sailors. And as part of their sailor duties, they had to carry the red curtain onstage. This was partly because the theater where we performed did not have a curtain. It was actually less like a theater and more like a high-ceilinged loft. And so Oleg and Dima carried the red curtain, which was about the size of a picnic blanket. They carried it onstage several times, in several different ways, during the course of the play. And it was like a reminder, for anyone who might have gotten lost, that this was theater. Theater, which is not life.

And so I stood backstage with Oleg and Dima, as they prepared to carry the curtain. The intermission curtain-carrying was different from the other times in that Oleg and Dima would stand there with it, and fall asleep. That is, they would hold the curtain between them, at shoulder height, in their respective right and left hands, and then they would close their eyes, and slowly bend from the waist, until eventually their heads were upside down, near their feet. But their hands would still be up high, holding the curtain. They would stand like that, and snore, until all the people were back in their seats.

And each night, during intermission, they stood backstage, and discussed the details of exactly how they were going to do this. They had this discussion in Russian. And I stood there, and listened to them without understanding, and thought of all the things I knew about them. That they were born and raised in Minsk, which is the capital of Belarus. That they came to New York two years ago. That they have been acting together since they were small. That Oleg told me, nodding at Dima, "I can be onstage with my eyes closed, and still, I know exactly what he is doing."

That they were part of a very close-knit theater troupe in Minsk, and it is their dream to save enough money to bring all the members of the troupe to New York. That the members of this theater troupe had this tradition, before they performed, of saying to each other, "I love you and forgive you everything." That Oleg and Dima, together, without their troupe, in a foreign country, still say that to each other before a show. That they embrace, and whisper it, into their respective right and left ears. I love you and forgive you everything. Ya tebya lyooblyoo ee vsyo tyebe proschayoo.

And I watched them, backstage, in the dark, at intermission, as they excitedly and wakefully talked about falling asleep in the light. And then they would walk away from me, and I would follow them until I came to the point where I was not allowed to follow them any further.

And then a small, gray tornado would begin to whirl in my chest, the kind you feel before you start to cry. But it wasn't because I was sad, it was because I was confused. I was so confused that I was confusion and her sister. And I would think of my father. And I would think of Oleg and Dima's friends in the theater troupe in Minsk. And I would think of all the people who were not here, who were missed. And then I would think, I am just one person. And then I would be confused. I would be in confusion, yes. I would be in something swirling, with the wind and rain coming out of my eyes. I would be in confusion. I would be in ecstasy, yes, with not knowing how many people one person is.

And I would look at Oleg and Dima, who would, by then, be standing and snoring, with their similar heads upside-down.

With their short blond hairs pulled into tiny wings, by gravity.

1.

Frank and I drove to Ohio for Thanksgiving. The plan was to drive to Youngstown first, see his mom, and then drive to Cleveland, to see mine. But then we got to his street, and we stopped first at the cemetery.

I had seen my dad's grave right after he was buried, when there was no marker. But since then, the cemetery lady had written to us, and said the marker was in.

The snow had just stopped falling. There was about a half-inch on the ground. I was pretty sure I could find the grave on my own, but I had called my mom beforehand, just to get extra directions. And so she told me to go in the front entrance, and take a right, and get out of the car at the first water fountain. Dad would be straight back from there, she said, right near the big oak tree, almost at the edge of the woods.

And so I started straight back, toward the edge of the woods, but I couldn't see any oak trees. There were pines. Tons of pines. And I would think I could spot an oak tree among the pines, in almost-winter. But I couldn't, so I started looking down at my feet. Because this was one of those cemeteries where the grave markers did not stick up. There were no tombstones. There were only brass plaques, set flush with the ground. But because of the snow, I could not see any plaques. I could not even see shadows or bumps in the snow, to hint where some plaques might be. So I started walking by sweeping my feet. And then whenever my toe would hit a plaque, I would wipe it with my boot, and try to read it.

And at first I did this casually. I had faith that, oak tree or no, I would find my dad. But after twenty minutes, there was nothing casual about it at all. I was looking for my dad. I was looking for my dad, who had once been a man, and was now a name. Then I was yelling "Frank!" I was yelling "Frank!" because he was still in the car, because it was freezing. I was yelling "Frank!" and remembering how he had told me, on the way in, how he and Kenny Bowes used to play here when they were kids. How they used to throw rocks at bees. How they used to torture whole dynasties of bees, and then run home for dinner. And I was stumbling around, kicking the snow, and I had my digital camera in my pocket, and I took it out, and I wanted to throw it. But instead I took a picture. I took a picture of there-is-no-oak-tree. I took a picture of there-is-no-dad-plaque. I took a picture of the snow and air and trees and sky around Frank. I took a picture of Frank walking toward me, in his puffy purple coat, and the green hat with the appliqued rabbit.

1.

I haven't told my mom I am pregnant yet. I am only five weeks pregnant, so I am waiting until things get a little more solid. Then I will tell her. And my brother.

The only person who knows is Frank. I told him when we were driving back to New York after Thanksgiving. I pretty much knew I was pregnant, but I wanted to be away from family before I checked. So I bought one of the kits, and then when we were at a stop along Route 80, I went into the BP station bathroom, and used it.

And afterward, I walked back to the car, biting my lips, and thought, how should I do this?

We were going to the place next door to the gas station, to get food. The parking lots between the two places were connected, so we could get from the gas station to the food place without going back on the road. The connection between the lots wasn't flat, though. It was a steep incline.

So I watched Frank's head, framed by the car window, as he drove us over the connection. And when the world in the window tilted up, that's when I said it.

And it was strange, how it didn't seem real, even after I said it, and then explained about the test.

And then the car started making these awful sounds, like the tail pipe, or the muffler, was dragging. And we stopped two times to look, but nothing was back there. And we still had four hours to go, so we just decided to go as fast as we could. And it was like there wasn't a baby inside me at all, just something chasing us.

1.

I called my mom yesterday.

"I found the gun," she said.

"The Luger?"

"Yes. It was in the closet in our bedroom."

"I thought you looked there already."

"I know, but I didn't look at the shelves on the floor. Just the ones near the ceiling."

"So that's where it was?"

"Yes, in a box with a lot of bullets. And of course, I called your brother immediately. And I didn't want to touch it, but he wanted me to describe it to him, so I had to go in the box and get it out and talk to him about it over the phone."

"And he said it was the Luger."

"Yes."

"Well, he must have been happy you found it. You know, he used to shoot that gun with Dad, when he was a kid."

"No, I didn't know that. I don't know anything about the histories."

My mother doesn't like guns. I wonder what kind of gun-mother I will be.

1.

Today I went to the obstetrician for the first time. She was recommended to me by the fertility doctor, who was full of congratulations when he found out I got pregnant without him.

And I was a little surprised when I first saw her, because she had these serious-looking scabs, or maybe they were scars, running down the left side of her face. She had put some makeup on them, so it was hard to tell. But after sitting in her warm, wood office, answering her very good questions, I forgot about them.

And after I answered all the questions, and asked some others, she led me to the examination room. And so I found myself back in the position, with my pants off, beside Mister

Ultrasound. And my obstetrician waited until she had the probe inside me to tell me why her face was so messed up.

"I was delivering babies all night," she said, a little sheepishly, "and I tripped and fell on the sidewalk."

I smiled at the ceiling. I loved her.

She turned the ultrasound screen so I could see it.

"There," she said. "That's the gestational sac."

It looked just like the follicles had looked, big and black, only instead of being a circle or oval, it was shaped like a lima bean.

She peered at the screen intently. She had told me she would be looking for a heartbeat, even though it was probably a little early.

She slid the probe out of me.

"Not yet," she said.

I put my clothes back on. I am supposed to come back in two weeks. I should see the heartbeat then, she said.

I walked down the hall to the elevator. I was inside my puffy coat and hat, inside my sweater and shirt and pants and socks and bra.

It was a long hall, with thick carpeting. I filled it with sound. Swish-swish. Swish-swish.

AFTERWORD

Writing *The Pharmacist's Mate* was a little like casting a spell on my own life. A few months after I finished it, two things that had merely been wishes suddenly, miraculously had tangible form: I could pat my pregnant belly with one hand while holding my first published book in the other.

But my developing baby and my newborn book were almost at odds with each other when it came time to consider another event: my book tour. It's not necessary for an author to tour the country, doing readings and interviews and generally promoting her book, of course, but as someone who has been wanting to tour since seventh grade (and having missed that opportunity with my college rock band), I was determined to go. After getting a blessing from my obstetrician, I was off. I was six months pregnant.

I toured the country for five weeks, visiting fifteen different cities. Traveling mostly alone, I carried not only my baby but my guitar, which I used to perform my girly version of AC/DC's "Hell's Bells" at readings. Keeping with the rock 'n roll theme, I named my tour "Amy Fusselman's Delicate Condition Tour" and kept a diary.

It was a little nerve-wracking to do so much traveling while pregnant, but the tour itself was actually a breeze compared to the process of getting ready for the tour. My anxiety was at a fever pitch a few days before leaving New York, as this diary entry attests:

> Even though I have all these things I need to do about the book, the little white book that feels like my baby right now, the baby that needs calls and e-mails, calls and e-mails, calls and trips to the post office, I have also grown out of all my bras, and am now larger than the largest size they sell in the J. Crew catalog, and without mail-order, my friends, I am lost. And so for two weeks now I have been walking around the house referring to myself as "TB," meaning "Tight Bra," telling Frank things like, "TB is going to the deli now" as I walk out the door, and this is probably part of some larger thing I need to explore about how, since I have become preg-nant, I've started to speak about myself in the third

person, I have been saying "Fatty needs another snack" or "The pregnant lady has to lie down now," and even though I don't know whether this is healthy or not, I think it honestly reflects how this bodily change is so enormous it's like it's happening to someone else.

And so yesterday even though I had all this other stuff to do I went to Macy's, and blindly grabbed about twenty bras in a size I previously associated only with porn stars, and then I got to the changing room line and there were fifteen women waiting there, and they had the sad, beleaguered air of women who had been waiting a long time, and were going to wait longer, and I just had a meltdown. I huffed over to the customer service counter and demanded that they open more dressing rooms or, I said, with my bed-head hair sticking straight up and my belly poking out of my orange hunting jacket, "I am going to start taking off my clothes right here." But the customer service lady just cocked an eyebrow at me and said sorry, but those were all the rooms they had, and so I demanded to see the manager, and she hooked a thumb in the manager's direction, and I went charging toward her with twenty hangers of red and pink bras slung over my neon orange shoulder, and when I found her, I made my speech again, and she chewed something, and ignored me. And by this time the third-person voice kicked in again, and I had a thought flit across my mind: "Fatty is having a breakdown." And having realized that, I couldn't stay there and fight any longer, and I threw my twisted-up bras on the counter and fled the lingerie department, the sixth floor, and then the entire stupid store, with my heart pounding.

Finally it was the day before I was going to leave New York for a month. I stayed up late packing, agonizing over what I was going to take with me. It was then that I realized that the prospect of carrying anything at all is a bit loaded, if you will, for a pregnant woman:

> Some women who have seen me pregnant say I am "carrying well." I am thinking of this as I pack for Toronto. After today I won't be home again for a month, so I have to take everything. Everything means my laptop, camera, phone, and all the wires for connecting and recharging them, my guitar, my vitamins and shower stuff, my wallet and date book, and my clothes. The decision to take the guitar was a big one. There is some weird German thing in my family where you get extra points for going on trips with as little luggage as possible. If I could, I would

be embarking on this tour with a wallet and two T-shirts. But now I have decided to drag the guitar across the country with me, even though it is huge and ungainly and I will be worried the whole time about whether or not I have to check it, because the case is not the sturdiest, and if I have to check it, it will get wrecked.

I am carrying well. I think when women say this, they mean that the lump on my stomach is sitting in a nice place, is maybe symmetrical in size and shape with the rest of my body.

So I have decided: I am taking a bike messenger bag full of clothes, a black vinyl computer bag, and the guitar case. I haven't yet tried to travel with all of this, and I am imagining how I will look shuffling through Newark Airport. I have a vague image of a Buddhist (?) statue of a many-armed god with a big belly. But that is a statue. I will be moving. I will be moving on top of the world that is also moving. I will be moving as the lump that is a boy inside me is moving, too.

I am afraid this is sounding like Bob Seger's "Turn the Page."

After visiting Toronto—where I asked a security guard at the Hockey Hall of Fame to take my picture in front of the Stanley Cup—I worked my way down to Ohio, so I could see my mother. She accompanied me to readings in Columbus and Cincinnati, where we stayed in a hotel together for the first time since I was small:

> I am in Cincinnati now, a town recently plagued by race riots. I am with my mother, who is 76 and afraid of big trucks on the highway, and loud noises, and forgetting her wallet, and having parts of the car suddenly and inexplicably fall off. I am ashamed of myself that I am letting her do any driving, but I am. She is only five feet tall, and sits on a pillow behind the wheel of the 4-wheel drive Honda, which used to be my dad's car, and which, when my dad was alive, she used to refuse to drive because she was afraid of it. But it's her car now.
>
> My mom is not doing much besides hanging out with me. I feel badly that I am not more fun, that I do not want to spend the day going to art museums or shopping, that all I really want to do is read the paper and take naps. But she says it's OK, it's like a vacation. We are not fighting. Every time she does something mildly irritating, I think of my dad. My mother is more precious to me now because she is a

person who knew my dad, and loved him. One day, I now know, there won't be any of these people left, including me.

Last night, in the hotel in Columbus, I woke up at 3 a.m. And I got up to pee, and came back, and my mother asked me if I was all right. And I was a little annoyed by that because I feel strange sleeping in the same room with her, it feels like a very weird intimacy I haven't experienced since I was small. And I wasn't sure if I wanted it. So I was trying very hard to preserve my Psychic Space, by which I mean that at night as we lie in the dark together, I try to pretend she is not there. And as I do this, I am hoping that she is doing the same thing. But then, you see, she speaks to me, and I realize that no, she is not.

And so I said something gruff and annoyed in response, like, "I'm fine, Mom," and tried to go back to sleep. And then in a very small voice, almost a whisper, she said, "I love you."

And I remembered this book I reread right before I started this tour, which is one of my favorite death books, called *Start the Conversation.* And in it, the author makes this case for why, when people die, you should not think of them as dead and gone forever, you should think of them as "out of town." She goes to great lengths to illustrate how much "dead" and "out of town" have in common. It's pretty convincing. And so I reread the book before the tour, and each time I have been tempted to get all weepy about my dad, I have been trying to sort of re-train my mind to think, "out of town, he's out of town." And sometimes, this actually works.

But in the middle of the night, in the Holiday Inn in Columbus, Ohio, with the medicinal smell of hotel-room cleansers still hanging in the air, and the alarming red glow from the oversized clock radio faintly illuminating the room, and my mom suddenly sitting up in bed and whispering that she loves me as I am lying there all prickly with my son silently floating in my womb, I realize: we are out of town now.

A week later, having passed through Chicago, Madison, and Minneapolis, I was in Seattle. I was ready to give myself a break by that time, and splurged on a swanky hotel room, where I discovered myself becoming very excited about a surprising amenity:

In Seattle I am staying at a hotel that provides pet goldfish. I request one, but he still hasn't arrived by the time I have to leave for the bookstore. When I come back afterward and turn the light on, though, he is there.

He is on the bedside table, in a bowl lined with multicolored pebbles and a green plastic plant. He is mostly white—silver, really—with two bright orange, crescent-shaped smudges along his gills, one on either side. And as soon as I see him I get very excited and call the front desk to ask where his food is, and how I should take care of him. But the young woman who answers the phone just laughs and says the hotel will do all that. My only job, she says, is to enjoy him.

And this is disappointing, because I had wanted to be able to interact with my goldfish, and feeding him would have been an easy way to do that. So now we are here together, him in his bowl of fruity pebbles, and me in the bed with the synthetic yellow, green, and pink spread. And I am delighting in him, I guess. Whenever I go to the bathroom and then come back to the bed I put my face up close to his bowl and growl, the way I do when I greet stranger's dogs on the street in New York. And I suppose he sees me, but he doesn't respond. The only thing I have noticed him responding to is when I turn the lights on. Then he swims around a lot. When the lights are off, he just hangs there.

And last night when I was asking the woman at the front desk about his food, I asked her where he went when he wasn't in my room, and she explained that the hotel keeps all the goldfish—over one hundred of them—in a big tank in the sub-basement, and the housekeeping ladies parcel them out in bowls depending on how many people ask for them.

And so this morning when I went downstairs for some coffee, I asked the front desk woman if she would let me see the big tank where all the goldfish are. And she giggled and said no, that that was in an area that was off-limits to guests. And I begged a little, but in what I thought was a nice way, and said, "Please, I love goldfish," and then she did not giggle, and just said: "No." And maybe this is because I am pregnant but it doesn't take much for me to see this whole goldfish situation as a metaphor for my relationship to every living thing, or more accurately, everything before it is living: there is a big tank in the sub-basement where all the fish are swimming together, but I am not allowed to see them like that. I can only see them one at a time, in their individual bowls, and then only if I am open, only if I ask. And even then, when one appears to me, it is not right for me to poke my finger in his water, even if it's just because I love him so much I want to hug his two-inch body for hours on end, and am frustrated that I cannot do that without killing him. No, my job is to take him as he is, in his decidedly uncuddly glass bowl, with his maddening silences. And not just to accept him like this, but to enjoy him.

And this is how I come face to face with my selfishness, because I don't know if I can enjoy this goldfish without knowing that he loves me, or if not loves me, then at least depends on me, i.e., swims up to my fingers greedily when I fill them with salty-smelling rainbow-colored flakes, and wiggle them over his head.

And this is disturbing to realize, that I have such difficulty enjoying anything that doesn't know I exist. Especially when I stop and think how big the world is, the world that is not even Japan or India, the world that is the room next door.

And I imagine what will happen after I leave here, and go away through the air, where my fish can't follow me. How the housekeeper will walk him over to the big tank and tip his bowl sideways. How he'll slip back into the familiar place, the spacious place, with his hundred brothers and mothers. How even if I stood there and tried, I would probably eventually lose sight of him.

After Seattle and Portland, I visited San Francisco, where I booked myself in a hotel on Fisherman's Wharf. I wanted to be there because San Francisco is where the S.S. *Jeremiah O'Brien,* one of the only surviving World War II Liberty Ships, has been turned into a museum. My dad had often talked about wanting to go to San Francisco to see it, but never had. I was happy to have the opportunity, and saw my dad immediately in the two old-timers in baseball hats and windbreakers who smiled happily as they greeted me at the top of the bridge.

I was shocked at how small the boat seemed. I had imagined a vast oceanliner, something more the size of an aircraft carrier, where you could be in the middle of the ocean and not feel scared the waves would swallow you. I was amazed at how my dad could have found such peace here, on this plain old not-so-very-big boat. I stood for a minute in front of the room that would have been his. I knew where it was because my dad had often pointed it out to me on a very detailed model of a Liberty Ship that he spent months constructing from a kit at home. It was on the upper deck because he had been a captain. On the *O'Brien* it was marked with a small sign that said PURSER. The sign hung from a chain suspended across the narrrow doorway. It swung slightly as the ship bobbed at the pier.

After San Francisco, I met up with Frank in Los Angeles for a week. It was fun to be out there, but I was starting to feel uncomfortable with how big I was getting, and was grateful, after a stop in Austin, Texas, to arrive back home.

I had planned the tour so that my reading in New York City would come at the end, after my travels. I arranged the event at my favorite New York City bookstore, Housing Works, and invited some special guests: the sea shanty singers I mention in the book, The New York Packet, and the actress/writer Colleen Werthmann. I envisioned a big celebration of the book, the now-completed tour, and the baby. After it was over, I planned on sitting out the remaining six weeks of my pregnancy on the couch, eating Popsicles.

But at 3 a.m. the night before the reading I went into labor. By the time I got to the hospital, I was one-and-a-half centimeters dilated. Concerned about the baby being born so early, my doctor decided that the best course of action was to try and stop my labor. I was given injections of Tributylene, a drug I knew well because it was given to my father in his last weeks. (Tributylene is a smooth-muscle relaxant. The bronchial tubes—like the uterus and the heart—are smooth muscle.) The hope was that the drug would slow the contractions.

Lying in the uncomfortable hospital bed, getting pumped full of Tributylene, I obviously thought of my dad. It seemed like a fitting end to the process that was *The Pharmacist's Mate*: what began with my dad in the hospital, trying not to die, would end with my lying in such similar circumstances, trying not to give birth.

The Tributylene slowed my contractions to the point where I was only having a few a day, so after three days, the doctors decided to send me home. I was to spend the remaining six weeks of my pregnancy on total bedrest, with a Tributylene pump attached to my thigh. Greatly relieved that the baby hadn't been born yet, I was willing to do anything.

I was home for only one day, though, when my water broke. Once your water breaks, there is no more stopping labor.

This time I came to the hospital seven-and-a-half centimeters dilated. Basically, I was almost ready to go. I was happy that I had gotten so far into my labor and hadn't needed any pain medication. My nurse asked me if I wanted an epidural as she wheeled me to the birthing room. I was OK right then, so I said no. In many birthing classes, they recommend that you not do this. You should ask for an epidural before you want one, they say, because there can be quite a wait, sometimes, before you get what you ask for. But I had gone into labor before our birthing class even started. We were supposed to start that week.

"Hurry!" I moaned to the nurse.

"Oh, you don't need to say you're sorry," she said sweetly, tapping away at the computer.

"No, I think she said *hurry,*" said Frank.

It was 7 a.m., in the middle of a shift change, and it took about an hour for the staff to locate the new anesthesia team. Once they found them, however, everything got better at once: my pain was greatly relieved, and my hard-of-hearing nurse was replaced by a new one, who, it turned out, was born in the same town as me, and went to my same elementary school. She held my one leg, and Frank held the other, and I pushed. Our son came out in a few minutes, and even though they said we should only expect him to be about four-and-a-half pounds, he was five pounds, nine ounces.

Right after he came out they put him on my chest. He did not seem upset. He wasn't crying. He looked right at me, like a good-natured and curious old man.

"I love you, I love you, I love you," I said. I wanted him to hear it as many times as possible before they took him away again.

We brought him home after three days, perfectly fine. We named him King, my father's middle name.

It was a shock, at first, having three of us at home. Frank kept saying, "We are a family now," like he was trying to get himself to believe it. At first I was weepy. Sometimes I still am. But then Frank says, "We're a family now, so can you please be happy all the time?" and I laugh.